W9-AOL-827

FESTIVE FOODS
FRANCE

Sylvia Goulding

CHELSEA
CLUBHOUSE
An Imprint of Chelsea House Publishers

Chelsea Clubhouse
An imprint of Chelsea House Publishers
132 West 31st Street
New York, NY 10001

Library of Congress Cataloging-in-Publication Data

Goulding, Sylvia.
 Festive foods / Sylvia Goulding. – 1st ed.
   v. cm.
 Includes bibliographical references and index.
 Contents: [1] China – [2] France – [3] Germany – [4] India – [5] Italy – [6] Japan – [7] Mexico – [8] United States.
 ISBN 978-0-7910-9751-9 (v. 1) – ISBN 978-0-7910-9752-6 (v. 2) – ISBN 978-0-7910-9756-4 (v. 3) – ISBN 978-0-7910-9757-1 (v. 4) – ISBN 978-0-7910-9753-3 (v. 5) – ISBN 978-0-7910-9754-0 (v. 6) – ISBN 978-0-7910-9755-7 (v. 7) – ISBN 978-0-7910-9758-8 (v. 8)
 1. Cookery, International. 2. Gardening. 3. Manners and customs. I. Title.
 TX725.A1G56 2008
 641.59–dc22

                    2007042722

Printed and bound in Dubai

10 9 8 7 6 5 4 3 2 1

For The Brown Reference Group plc.:
Project Editor: Sylvia Goulding
Cooking Editor: Angelika Ilies
Contributors: Jacqueline Fortey, Sylvia Goulding
Photographers: Klaus Arras, Emanuelle Morgan
Cartographer: Darren Awuah
Art Editor: Paula Keogh
Illustrator: Jo Gracie
Picture Researcher: Mike Goulding
Managing Editor: Bridget Giles
Production Director: Alastair Gourlay
Editorial Director: Lindsey Lowe
Children's Publisher: Anne O'Daly

Photographic Credits:
Front and Back Cover: Klaus Arras
Pierre-Jérôme Atger: 31; **Fotolia:** 6; **Mike Goulding:** 13, 20, 22, 37, 38; **iStock:** title page, 3, 4, 14, 30, 35, 39; **Nathalie Le Marrec:** 28; **Shutterstock:** 5, 7, 8, 9, 10, 12, 13, 21, 23, 24, 29, 30, 36

With thanks to models:
Caspar, Ella, Eugene, Felix, Jeremy, Phoebe

Cooking Editor
Angelika Ilies has always been interested in cookery and other countries. She studied nutritional sciences in college. She has lived in the United States, England, and Germany. She has also traveled extensively and collected international recipes on her journeys. Angelika has written more than 70 cookbooks and cooking card series. She currently lives in Frankfurt, Germany, with her two children and has spent much time researching children's nutrition. Both children regularly cook with their mother.

Contents

let's
START COOKING

Cooking is fun—you learn about different ingredients and cooking methods, you find out how things taste, and you can serve a meal to your family and friends that you have cooked yourself! Some of the recipes in this book have steps that need adult help—ask a parent or other adult if they will be your kitchen assistant while you cook a meal.

This line tells you how many people the meal will feed.

In this box, you find out which ingredients you need for your meal.

WHAT YOU NEED:

SERVES 4 PEOPLE:

2¼ cups white rice
4 eggs, beaten
light soy sauce
4 tablespoons
   groundnut or
   soy oil
2 green onions
⅛ cup peeled shrimps
⅓ cup ham
⅓ cup green peas

Check before you start that you have everything you need. Get all the ingredients ready before you start cooking.

◁ Fresh fruits or vegetables are ripe when they have a strong aroma. Whenever I can, I like to feel and smell a fruit or vegetable before I buy it.

! WHEN TO GET help

Most cooking involves cutting ingredients and heating them in some way, whether frying, boiling, or cooking in the oven. Each time you see this exclamation mark, be extra careful as you cook and make sure your adult kitchen assistant is around to help.

For many meals you need to chop an onion. First cut off a thin slice at both ends. Pull off the peel. Cut the onion in half from end to end. Put one half with the cut side down on the chopping board. Hold it with one hand and cut end-to-end slices with the other hand. Hold the slices together and cut across the slices to make small cubes. Make sure you do not cut yourself!

Other recipes in this book use fresh garlic. Break a whole head of garlic into separate cloves. Cut the top and the bottom off each clove, and pull off the papery skin. Now you can either chop the garlic clove with a sharp knife, or you can use a garlic crusher to squeeze the garlic directly into the skillet or saucepan. If you are worried about garlic breath, chew some parsley.

A **barbecue** is not essential, but in the summer French people often like to cook a meal outdoors.

With a **garlic crusher** you can crush garlic into a purée for sauces, when you do not want to add garlic pieces.

Oil and vinegar, together with garlic, mustard, salt, and pepper, make a typical French salad dressing called *vinaigrette*.

A cast-iron **Dutch oven** or casserole dish is used for making stews and roasts. It has a tight-fitting lid.

A trip around
FRANCE

France is the largest country in western Europe and is about twice the size of Colorado. It is famed for its beautiful countryside, rich culture, and delicious food.

France is nicknamed the "hexagon" because it fits into a six-sided shape. An ocean and a sea form three of its sides. The coastline has rugged cliffs, windswept dunes, sandy beaches, and rocky coves. In the south, the coast meets the warm Mediterranean Sea. The narrow English Channel separates northern France from England.

Belgium and Luxembourg are France's northern neighbors. Germany and Switzerland are on the east side, and Italy is to the southeast. France's southwestern border with Spain runs through the Pyrenees mountain range.

France has mostly fairly cool winters and mild summers. But the south is much warmer and the east much colder than the rest of the country.

The north

The northwest regions of Normandy and Brittany have lovely beaches, cliffs, bays, and harbors. Wide, flat plains and gentle hills stretch across much of northern France. They form an area around the Seine River called the Paris Basin. Toward the country's north

◁ *More than 63 million people* live in France. Its main immigrant groups consist of southern and eastern Europeans, North Africans, and Arabs.

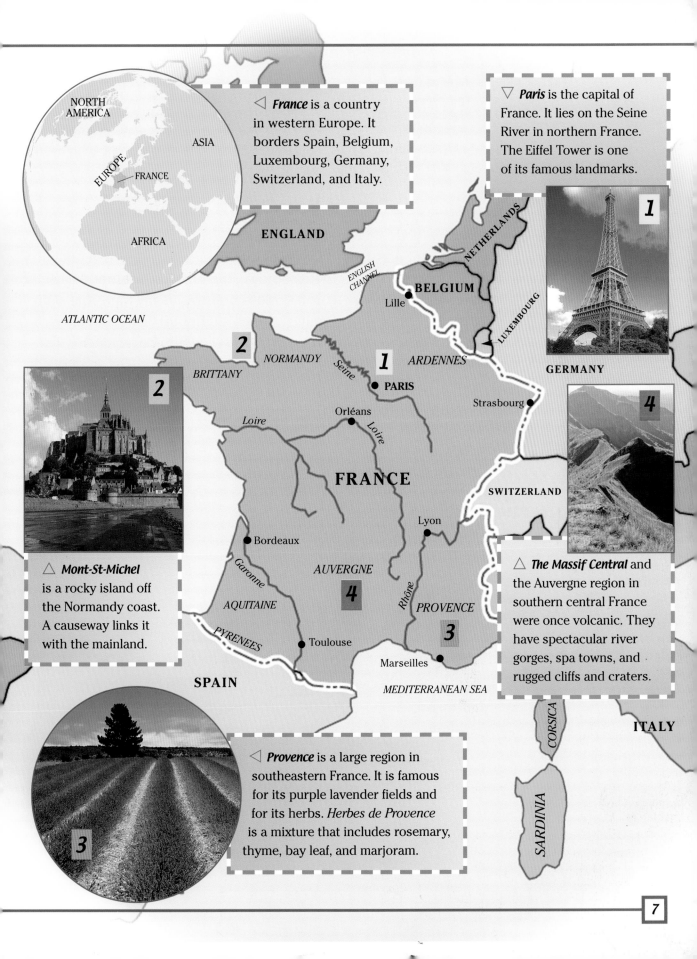

NORTH AMERICA

ASIA

EUROPE — FRANCE

AFRICA

ATLANTIC OCEAN

◁ **France** is a country in western Europe. It borders Spain, Belgium, Luxembourg, Germany, Switzerland, and Italy.

▽ **Paris** is the capital of France. It lies on the Seine River in northern France. The Eiffel Tower is one of its famous landmarks.

1

ENGLAND

ENGLISH CHANNEL

NETHERLANDS

Lille

BELGIUM

LUXEMBOURG

GERMANY

2

NORMANDY

BRITTANY

Seine

1

ARDENNES

● **PARIS**

Strasbourg ●

2

Orléans ●

Loire

Loire

FRANCE

4

SWITZERLAND

Lyon ●

△ **Mont-St-Michel** is a rocky island off the Normandy coast. A causeway links it with the mainland.

Loire

● Bordeaux

Garonne

AUVERGNE

4

Rhône

PROVENCE

3

△ **The Massif Central** and the Auvergne region in southern central France were once volcanic. They have spectacular river gorges, spa towns, and rugged cliffs and craters.

AQUITAINE

PYRENEES

Toulouse ●

Marseilles ●

SPAIN

MEDITERRANEAN SEA

CORSICA

ITALY

◁ **Provence** is a large region in southeastern France. It is famous for its purple lavender fields and for its herbs. *Herbes de Provence* is a mixture that includes rosemary, thyme, bay leaf, and marjoram.

3

SARDINIA

and eastern borders, the landscape changes. The Ardennes region is part of a forest plateau with ridges and deep valleys. Farther east, the Vosges mountains stretch along the west bank of the Rhine River.

Central France

Two famous wine-growing regions lie south of the Paris Basin. The rich province of Burgundy to the east stretches down to the large city of Lyons. To the west, the Loire Valley is known for its wine and splendid castles.

Below these regions lies the Massif Central. This huge plateau makes up nearly one-fifth of France's total area. The area has a dramatic landscape that was created by volcanic eruptions long ago. It is the source of several rivers, including the Dordogne, the Loire, the Lot, and the Tarn. The Tarn and the Aveyron rivers have worn away limestone rocks to form deep gorges. They attract rock climbers, hikers, and white-water rafters.

Farther east, the Rhône River flows from north to south through a wide valley. Beyond the river to the east are the snowy peaks of the French Alps. Here is Europe's highest mountain, Mont Blanc (15,780 feet).

Southern France

The Garonne River flows northwest from the Pyrenees into the huge estuary (river mouth) at Bordeaux. This trading port is at the center of a world-famous region for wine. Vast sand dunes stretch southward along the Atlantic coast. This area contains huge pine trees, ponds, marshes, and moors. The countryside in Poitou and Aquitaine is fairly flat until it

▽ **Château de Chambord** is the largest of the magnificent castles in the Loire Valley. The château is 140 yards long. It has 440 rooms, 365 fireplaces, 13 staircases, and stables for 1,200 horses. It stands in a park that is surrounded by a 22-mile-long wall.

reaches the craggy peaks of the Pyrenees. This mountain range runs across southwest France almost to the Mediterranean. Bears and mountain goats live here.

Sunny Provence in the southeast has many resorts. Flamingos wade and white horses roam in the salt marshes of the Camargue, west of Marseilles. In the east the land rises sharply into the Alpes-Maritimes. These mountains run along the beautiful Côte d'Azur (Azure Coast).

▽ *The town of Luzech* in the southwest stands in one of many loops made by the Lot River. The river meanders (follows a winding and turning course) past hilltops planted with vines.

ALL SORTS OF CHÂTEAUX

France has about 40,000 castles, or châteaux. Some are magnificent and huge, but some look just like simple farmhouses. Any building on a wine estate can call itself a château—whether it has lots of turrets or not!

The food we grow in
FRANCE

France is the most important farming country in Western Europe. About two-thirds of the country is farmland.

*T*he largest French farms are on the northern plains and in the west. Near Calais, people grow potatoes and sugarbeet. The Paris Basin has very fertile soil. Here, farmers grow wheat, barley, corn, and peas. In Normandy, on the northwest coast, herds of cows graze in the fields. Their milk is made into cream, cheese, and butter. Lamb is raised on salt marshes near the coast, and apples are grown to make into cider.

The landscape in Champagne is covered with vines growing grapes for sparkling wine. There are also vineyards in Alsace-Lorraine, around the Vosges mountains. People here grow hops, which are used for brewing beer. Local specialties are hams, soft cheese, sauerkraut (pickled cabbage), and cakes. The orchards and market gardens are filled with cherry trees, blueberry bushes, and raspberry canes.

Central France

The rocky regions of the Massif Central in the south are too bleak to grow many crops. But the Loire Valley is sometimes called the "Garden of France," because fruit and vegetables thrive

in its rich soil. A meal in a local restaurant might include freshwater fish followed by cheese and *tarte tatin* (apple tart). Caves alongside the Loire River are cool and dark —perfect for growing mushrooms.

In the Rhône Valley, peaches, apricots, plums, and tomatoes are grown on small farms. The beautiful region of Burgundy is famous for its great wines and hearty beef stews. The town of Bresse advertises its produce with a giant metal chicken by the side of the road—chickens here are supposed to be the tastiest in the world.

Dijon is the home of a strong mustard. It was once made from seed grown in the fields around Dijon, but now most mustard seed is imported from Canada. The city of Lyon is known as a center for food lovers.

There are lush green meadows in the Franche-Comté region, along the Swiss border. Here cowbells chime as brown and white cows munch the grass. Cheese makers mature large drums of nutty Comté cheese from their milk. This cheese is good for melting in soups, gratins, and other baked dishes. In the mountains, people make smoked sausages and hams.

A CHEESE A DAY

French people make about 400 different cheeses. That's more than a different cheese for every single day of the year!

Southwestern France

In the southwest, the local produce includes many duck and goose products, such as pâtés, goose gizzards (a second stomach), and duck breasts. Both birds are preserved in their own fat; this is called *confit*. Goose fat is also used to cook many dishes.

In the Perigord and Quercy regions, rare strong-smelling fungi called truffles grow under trees, particularly oaks. Nuts from walnut groves are used to make walnut oil. Fields of sunflowers are also grown to make oil.

Aquitaine, along the Atlantic, has dairy farms, fruit orchards, and market gardens. The Basque capital, Bayonne, is famous for its hams. In Languedoc-Roussillon, market gardeners grow delicious pitted fruits, such as peaches and apricots.

Southeastern France

Farmers keep sheep on the wetlands of the Camargue. The scent of herbs and lavender is in the air in neighboring Provence. Farmers also grow garlic, peppers, tomatoes, eggplants, olives, and fennel. These ingredients appear in local dishes, such as a vegetable stew called *ratatouille*, in *salade Niçoise*, and in *aïoli*, vegetables with a garlic mayonnaise.

Fishing

France is one of the largest fishing nations in the European Union. Small boats fish in the waters around Brittany and along the Mediterranean coast. Larger boats set sail for longer trips from ports such as Concarneau in Brittany and Boulogne in the north. Shellfish, especially oysters, scallops, and clams, are farmed and collected in the bays of Brittany. The Bassin d'Arcachon south of Bordeaux is another area where oysters are farmed. In Provence, a fish stew called *bouillabaisse* is a specialty.

◁ *Geese and ducks* are raised in southwestern France. They are roasted, preserved in their own fat, cured or smoked like hams, made into pâté and sausages, or stewed in wine. Often they are served with fruits—orange, prunes, or grapefruits.

▽ **Fishing boats** lie anchored in a harbor in Corsica. Fishers catch sea urchins, which are eaten raw, gold bream, St. Pierre-fish, and red barbel. Fish are often served grilled. Delicacies include perch and lobster.

RURAL FRANCE

While most French people live in towns, the countryside is still a lively place. Even if people work in an office, they often have some land. People grow fruits and vegetables in their gardens, and they may also keep a few chickens and some sheep.

let's make...
ALSACE
ONION TART

This savory open tart comes from the Alsace region in eastern France. Grandma used the onions from her own garden to make it, and she always served it hot.

WHAT YOU NEED:

MAKES 6 PORTIONS:

2 cups all-purpose flour	1 egg
½ teaspoon salt	1⅔ cup chilled butter

FOR THE TOPPING:

1 lb 5 ounces onions	1 cup milk
1 stick butter	2 egg yolks
salt, black pepper	1 cup heavy cream
paprika	4 ounces lean smoked ham
2 tablespoons flour	4 ounces Gruyère cheese

PLUS:

1 quiche dish, 11 inches wide

◁ This tart makes a nice light lunch or supper. We eat it with a simple green salad, some crusty bread, and a glass of juice.

EASY onion tart

Instead of making the dough yourself, you could also use ready-made pastry. Choose a puff pastry for a change, or try making this tart with a pizza base. For the topping you could add some chopped fresh parsley, or use a cream cheese instead of the milk and heavy cream.

1 Knead together the ingredients for the dough. Shape it into a ball and wrap it in plastic wrap. Chill for about 1 hour. Meanwhile peel the onions and cut them into very thin slices. Separate the slices into rings.

2 Melt half the butter in a saucepan. Add the onion rings and fry and stir for 3 minutes, until they are golden. Season with salt, pepper, and paprika.

3 Melt the rest of the butter in a second saucepan. Tip in the flour, stir and fry until it is golden. Continue stirring, while you add the milk, a little at a time. Cook over low heat for about 5 minutes. Take the saucepan off the heat. Stir in the egg yolks and the cream, and then the onions.

4 Heat the oven to 400°F. Knead the dough again, then roll it out thinly. Line the quiche dish with the dough. Cut off the overlap.

5 Spread the onion mixture onto the dough. Chop the ham into cubes and grate the cheese. Sprinkle the tart with both. Bake in the oven for 40 minutes. Allow the tart to rest for 10 minutes before cutting.

let's make...
POTATO GRATIN

Gratin dauphinois (say "gra-taing dau-fee-nwah") is a specialty from Grenoble, in the foothills of the Alps. These scalloped potatoes are cooked until they are golden and crusty.

WHAT YOU NEED:

SERVES 3-4 PEOPLE:

- 1 lb waxy potatoes, for example Yukon Gold
- 2 garlic cloves
- 2 tablespoons butter (plus some more to grease the aluminum foil)
- 3 eggs
- 1⅔ cup whipping cream or milk
- salt, white pepper

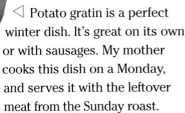

◁ Potato gratin is a perfect winter dish. It's great on its own or with sausages. My mother cooks this dish on a Monday, and serves it with the leftover meat from the Sunday roast.

WHAT'S THIS: gratin?

Almost any vegetable can be made into a gratin—a dish with cream or cheese that is cooked in the oven to get a crust. Potatoes are often included.

MY TIP

Choose potatoes that have about the same size and shape so they all cook evenly.

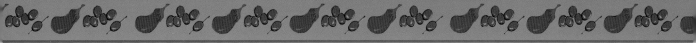

1 Heat the oven to 400°F. Peel the potatoes, wash them, and cut them into thin slices.

4 In a bowl, whisk together the eggs with the cream or milk. Season with plenty of salt and pepper. Pour the mixture over the potatoes.

5 Grease a sheet of aluminum foil with butter, then use it to cover the dish. Bake the potatoes for about 20 minutes. !

2 Peel and finely chop the onion *(see page 5)*. Melt the butter in a skillet until it foams. Add the onion and fry it until it is transparent (see-through). Empty the skillet into a gratin dish with a flat bottom. Spread the onion and butter around in the dish to grease it. !

3 Arrange the potato slices in the dish in overlapping circles.

6 Take off the foil and bake the gratin for 30 to 40 minutes more, until the potatoes start to look golden brown. Check that the potatoes are done—if you stick in a sharp knife they should feel just about soft. !

let's make...
SALADE NIÇOISE

A basket of sun-ripened vegetables goes into this salad from the town of Nice, in southern France. Nice is nice, but it's pronounced "nees" and the salad is a "salard nee-swahrze."

WHAT YOU NEED:

SERVES 4 PEOPLE:

½ lb small potatoes
9 ounces green beans
salt, black pepper
1 onion
4 tomatoes
 1 small green bell pepper
  ½ cucumber

1 can tuna in natural
 juice (6 ounces)
½ lettuce
10 black olives
4 twigs basil

FOR THE DRESSING:

4 tablespoons red wine
 vinegar
1 garlic clove
1 teaspoon mustard
6 tablespoons
 olive oil

◁ I bought all the ingredients for this salad in the market. Now I'll make this refreshing lunch.

MY TIP

Try adding some hard-boiled eggs. Boil the eggs in their shells in hot water for about 8 minutes. Refresh them under cold water, shell them when they're cold enough to touch, then cut each egg into fourths and add.

1 Wash the potatoes and boil them in their skins in a little water for about 15–20 minutes until they are only just soft. Drain and allow to cool, then peel and slice the potatoes. **!**

2 Wash and trim the beans. Cook them in salted water for 10 minutes over low heat. Drain, then rinse them under cold water. Drain in a sieve.

3 Peel and halve the onion, then cut it into thin half-moons. Separate these. Wash the tomatoes and cut them into eighths. Remove the stem ends. Wash, trim, halve, and deseed the bell pepper, then cut it into strips. **!**

4 Peel the cucumber and halve it lengthways. Cut into half-moons. Drain the tuna. Wash the lettuce, shake it dry, and tear it into smaller pieces.

5 In a bowl, combine the vinegar and mustard. Press in the garlic. Whisk in the olive oil, a little at a time, until you have a creamy dressing.

6 Put all the vegetables into the bowl and turn them with spoons until they are coated all over. Sprinkle in the olives and some basil leaves.

How we celebrate in
FRANCE

People in France enjoy eleven national holidays. Most are celebrated with big meals, dances, and fireworks.

French holidays celebrate important days in the country's history, such as the French Revolution in 1789, Armistice (peace) after World War I in 1918, and Victory (from German rule) after World War II in 1945. Other French holidays are Christian celebrations, including Easter, Whitsun, and Christmas.

Bastille Day

Bastille Day is the French National Holiday, or la Fête Nationale. It is also known by its date, *Quatorze Juillet*—July 14. Bastille Day is a bit like Independence Day in the United States. The festival remembers the events of July 14, 1789. On that day, people stormed the Bastille prison in Paris. They were protesting against the rule of a corrupt king and queen. Their protest was the start of the French Revolution.

▷ **Honorary citizens** sport the national flag for a ceremony in a small town on Bastille Day, July 14. A band plays the national anthem, which is known as the Marseillaise. Sometimes a recording of the anthem is played. Then people shout: "Vive la France!" and continue with the festivities.

▷ **Spectacular fireworks** are part of most celebrations in France. There are always huge fireworks for Bastille Day on July 14, but you can also enjoy fireworks during every village fête. Many people also buy fireworks to celebrate a birthday or other family occasion.

Today, the day is marked by a military parade in Paris. The president leads the parade, and jets fly overhead in formation. They blaze the national colors: blue, white, and red. In smaller towns, there are similar ceremonies, often at war memorials. During the day there are fairs and fun events all over France. At night, people enjoy large feasts and dances until the fireworks at midnight.

MUSIC FOR FREE

June 21 is the Fête de la Musique. All over France, musicians play for free in the streets. You can hear rock, reggae, country, techno, rap, classical, and also traditional French songs, or chansons.

Le Tour

The Tour de France is a huge cycle race around France. It takes three weeks to complete. Often the Tour also visits neighboring countries, such as Belgium or England across the Channel. While the cycle race is not a national holiday, many people are given the day off by their employers when the race passes through their town or village.

People line the roads and find the best spot to stand hours before the Tour passes. This is because the "Caravane" arrives before the cyclists. The Caravane is a publicity convoy of about 300 cars. They advertise anything from savings banks to mobile phones, and throw some ten million samples or gifts, such as keyrings, to the spectators. After the Caravane has gone, the cyclists and their support vehicles pass, and then everyone has a barbecue or a party.

▽ **The "Caravane"** is a convoy of advertising cars or floats that runs for about one hour before the cyclists in the Tour de France.

Toussaint

Toussaint is All Saints' Day, on November 1. This Catholic holiday celebrates all the saints who do not have their own saint's day at one time. It is also a day to remember the departed; people clean and decorate the graves of their dead. Today, typical Halloween customs are also celebrated in France. French children trick-or-treat, carve jack-o'-lanterns, and dress up in scary costumes.

1 Stir together the eggs, milk, flour, and sugar to make a batter. Heat the butter in a small skillet until it is golden brown and stir it into the mixture. Set the batter aside.

2 To make the sauce, scrub the oranges under hot water and pat them dry. With a potato peeler, pare off the zest of one orange in thin strips. Squeeze out the juice. In a saucepan, cook the zest, juice, and sugar over high heat to make a thin syrup.

3 Peel the remaining two oranges. Also completely peel off the white inner skins. With a sharp knife, cut out the orange slices between their thin skins. Catch the juice.

4 In two nonstick skillets melt some of the butter until it foams. Pour in 1 ladleful of batter. Turn the skillet so the batter covers the whole base. Fry the crêpe for 1 minute, then carefully turn it over with a wooden spatula. Now fry the other side for only about 30 seconds.

5 Place the finished crêpes on a rack and cover them with a clean cloth. Fry six more crêpes as above.

6 Place the orange slices on the crêpes and fold the crêpes over. Put the crêpes back into the skillets, pour over the syrup and heat through for 1 minute.

How we celebrate at home in
FRANCE

In France people love their food. To celebrate a personal event, such as a birthday or a wedding, they will spare no money or effort to prepare a grand celebratory meal. Such meals are also a way of thanking friends and neighbors for their help during the harvest, for example picking grapes.

▽ *Family banquets* for special occasions such as weddings often take place in people's own homes. Long tables and benches are set out in the yard and covered with white tablecloths. Everyone joins in. The meals often last for many hours, and the dancing and the music carry on through the night.

Festive meals

A traditional French meal has many courses. The meal starts with pre-dinner drinks called *aperitif* and savory snacks or olives. Then people sit down and have the first course, which is often a soup, for example onion soup. After that they have a plate of ham, pâté, and cold meats called *charcuterie*, melon, or a seafood salad. This is followed by the *entrée*, a main course, often of fish. Afterward there is the main meat course, for example duck breast, roast meat, a stew, or a steak. The vegetables often follow separately, after the meat. Then there will be a green salad, to give a fresh taste. Finally, a plate of different cheeses is followed by dessert. *Bon appetit!*

Christmas

Families celebrate Christmas together with a late and very festive meal on Christmas Eve. Many homes have a Christmas tree and a crèche (model of the Nativity scene). Santa Claus is known in France as Père Noël. He arrives late at night, when young children are already asleep. Père Noël leaves the gifts next to the tree, in the shoes, or in Christmas stockings. Religious people go to midnight mass. The churches are beautifully lit and the bells ring out Christmas carols.

▷ **Christmas decorations** can be seen on most shops, as in this famous department store in Paris. But aside from having a real Christmas tree with candles, people do not normally decorate their homes for Christmas.

◁ *Lilies of-the-valley* are the flowers that people give each other on May 1, as a token of happiness. Many flowers link to special days: on November 1, chrysanthemums are laid on graves—these flowers should never be given as a gift.

Weddings

On the day of the wedding, the bridegroom picks up his future wife from her home. The bride is dressed in a beautiful white gown, and she wears a crown and flowers in her hair. After the church ceremony, guests may shower the bride with rice—to wish her many children. She then has to cut a white ribbon that is stretched across the street by children.

After the wedding there is, of course, a big feast for family and friends. The couple drink a toast from a double-handled glass, called

Mother's Day

This day is celebrated on the last Sunday in May. But if that date is also Whit Sunday, it is celebrated on the first Sunday in June instead. On this day, children tell their mother how much she is loved and needed. They give her gifts they have made at school and a bouquet of flowers. It is also the day when Maman does not have to cook—the children either cook a nice meal for her at home or they take her out for a meal in a restaurant.

▷ *A croquembouche wedding cake* is a high cone of cream-filled buns or profiteroles. It is beautifully decorated with long caramel or chocolate threads, flowers, and ribbons. The word *croquembouche* means "crunch in the mouth."

the *coupe de mariage*, or marriage cup. The French wedding cake is known as *croquembouche*. It is a pyramid of glazed cream-filled pastry buns. The bride and bridegroom have to try and kiss over the top of the pyramid. This symbolizes a long and happy life together.

Village fêtes

In many rural areas, people used to celebrate a successful vegetable harvest by having a meal together in the village. Everyone brought their own plates and cutlery, and they also brought some food or drink along.

Today, these fêtes are still celebrated in many parts of France. While people still have to bring their own implements, the meals have become sit-down dinners for 300 or more people. The fêtes themselves have also become larger—often they last for four days.

There are usually one or several nights for dancing. The music includes rock and pop, but also traditional French folk music, which is known as *musette* and often played on the accordion. Other regular events may include pétanque competitions, loft sales, exhibitions of art and local crafts, carriage rides, cooking competitions, and traditional games.

◁ *A communal meal* at the village fête in the tiny hamlet of Les Arques in southwestern France. After the meal, people dance to the music until midnight, then they stop to watch the fireworks.

MANY HAPPY RETURNS

The longest life we know of for sure was that of Jeanne Calment of France (1875-1997). She was 122 years old when she died. She was very healthy and still rode a bicycle when she was aged 100!

let's make...
DUCK BREAST

This classic dish from southwestern France is a favorite meal to serve for special family occasions, such as birthdays, jubilees, and other events. It's easy to cook and truly delicious.

WHAT YOU NEED:

SERVES 4 PEOPLE:

3 tablespoons lemon juice
2 tablespoons runny honey
salt, black pepper
2 duck breast fillets (about
   10 ounces each)
2 tablespoons cooking oil
a handful of shallots, diced

◁ Et voilà! The best duck breast ever. My sister doesn't like the skin so she leaves it on her plate. But don't skin the meat before cooking as the skin flavors the duck.

MY TIP

You can also cook the duck in the oven. Prick the duck skin several times with a fork. Place the duck skin side down on a rack and roast it in the oven at 400°F for about 20–30 minutes. Put a dish under the duck to collect the fat that runs off. Save the fat for roasting potatoes.

1 In a bowl, stir together the lemon juice, honey, salt, and pepper. Wash the duck breasts under cold water and pat them dry. Place them in a large ovenproof dish and rub them all over with the marinade. Cover the dish with plastic wrap and chill it in the fridge for at least 2 hours.

4 Put the duck breasts on a serving platter, cover, and keep them warm in the oven (at 200°F). **!**

5 Peel and slice the shallots. Fry them in the skillet over medium heat until they look glassy. Pour in 5 tablespoons water. Using a wooden spoon, loosen the meat juices in the skillet. Add the marinade. Bring the sauce to a boil and season it with salt and pepper. **!**

2 Take the fillets out of the marinade and pat them dry. Set the marinade aside. Heat the oven to 200°F.

3 In a skillet, heat the oil over medium heat. Place the fillets in the skillet with the skin side down and fry them for about 7 minutes. Turn them over and fry for a further 5–7 minutes.

6 Slice the duck breast crossways into thin slices and fan these out on the serving platter. Pour over a little of the sauce and serve.

let's make...
CHOCOLATE MOUSSE

Most people I know like chocolate. In fact, everyone I know likes chocolate. And this mousse is the most heavenly dessert. Unfortunately, Mom only makes it for special occasions!

WHAT YOU NEED:

SERVES 4-6 PEOPLE:

5 ounces aromatic chocolate (milk chocolate, bitter chocolate, or half of each)
2 large eggs
2 tablespoons confectioners' sugar
½ cup whipping cream or heavy cream
1 teaspoon vanilla extract
whipped cream and cocoa powder to serve

◁ The great thing about making chocolate mousse is that I get to lick the bowl when I'm done!

WHAT SORT OF chocolate?

You can choose any chocolate you like. Try making the mousse (which is pronounced moose) with a white chocolate or a chocolate with orange or mint flavors.

MY TIP

Melt chocolate in the microwave on medium for 1½–4 minutes until it is shiny, then stir.

1 On a cutting board, roughly chop the chocolate with a large knife. Put the chocolate into a small bowl. Fill some water into a saucepan that is slightly larger than the bowl and bring it to a boil. **!**

2 Place the bowl in the saucepan. Stir the chocolate all the time as it melts. Remove the pan from the heat.

3 Carefully separate the eggs. With a handheld whisk, beat the egg whites until stiff. Slowly sprinkle in the sugar while you whisk. Chill the stiff egg whites in the fridge. Now whisk the cream until stiff, then chill it.

4 In a large bowl, whisk the egg yolks and the vanilla extract with a clean whisk until they are creamy. Slowly stir in the melted chocolate.

5 Place the stiff cream on top of the chocolate mixture. Stir it in gently with a whisk.

6 Now place the stiff egg whites on top. Gently mix them into the mousse by pulling a spoon through both in a figure-eight. Don't mix or whisk, or the whole mousse will collapse. Chill the mousse in the fridge for at least 3 hours. Spoon it into glasses, top with whipped cream, and sprinkle with some cocoa powder.

How we live in
FRANCE

Most French people live in towns, but the countryside is very important. There is a big difference between life in Paris and other large towns and life in the "provinces."

City life

Parisians and other people in French cities, work hard and are often rushed. These days, they may have a sandwich next to their computers rather than enjoying a traditional two-hour lunch break. Despite its excellent transportation system, Paris experiences great traffic problems. Its circular highway, the Périphérique, is often jammed. In summer, pollution from the cars creates a cloud of smog above the larger towns.

In the city, French people are interested in fashion. Paris is one of the fashion centers of the world, and there are great fashion shops, or boutiques, in all the cities.

▽ *French beaches*, such as this one in Cassis in southern France, attract French vacationers as well as foreign visitors.

△ *Antiques fairs* are a national passion. Throughout the year and in every town and village, there are numerous antiques fairs, flea markets, or loft sales. Popular items to sell—and buy—are furniture, jewelry, books, old postcards, glasses, and dishes.

PARDON?

Most French people speak standard French, but there are also many local dialects. Older people may sometimes be hard to understand because they speak "patois," their rural dialect.

Vacations

Traditionally, people in France take all their vacations at one time. They take leave for the whole of the month of July or August. In the past, most people spent their vacations in France, on the coast or in the countryside. Many French families have relatives in the countryside, and some wealthier people have second homes there. Today, many people vacation abroad. They go to French islands such as Martinique or French-speaking islands such as Mauritius. In winter they go to North Africa or they ski in the French Alps.

If a holiday falls in the middle of the week, people often take one or two "bridge days." That is, they take the days in between the weekend and the holiday off too, to make a long weekend.

△ **Pétanque** is a boules game similar to English lawn bowling and Italian boccia. It is played by millions of French people of all ages on vacation. The game comes from the southern port of Marseilles and is now popular throughout the country.

Pastimes

The most popular sports in France are rugby and soccer, and most people support both their local and the national teams. The national teams are known as "les bleus," the blues, after their team color. French sportsmen and women also excel at sailing, automobile racing, judo, and fencing. The varied countryside and climate allow people to ski in the Alps, to swim and sail anywhere along the coasts, and to fish, hike, explore caves, and rock climb throughout the center of the country. Not everyone is active, though. French children, like those elsewhere, also spend many hours playing computer games, watching TV, and on the Internet.

Going to school

Babies and young children are cared for in day centers. After that, they go to a *maternelle*, or preschool. They start elementary school when they are six years old. There they learn reading, writing, math, history, and geography. From eleven to fourteen they visit *collège*, where they learn two foreign languages and computer

studies. The *lycée* is the last stage before university. It finishes with an exam known as *le bac*, similar to a U.S. high school diploma.

At lunchtime, children have a two-hour break. They go home to eat or eat at the school *cantine*. Their meals may include exotic foods such as snails or octopus as well as cheeses and desserts. There is no school on Wednesdays, but many pupils have to go to school on Saturday mornings.

State schools are secular in France, which means they are not religious. This has caused problems for Muslim girls, who are not allowed to wear their headscarves in class.

▽ **The Sorbonne** is one of thirteen universities in Paris and one of the best in France. To go to university, students have to pass their *bac*. They need to get at least 10 points out of 20.

SORBONNE

UNIVERSITE DE PARIS

FRENCH AROUND THE WORLD

French is a main language in Bénin, Burkina Faso, Central African Republic, both Congos, Côte d'Ivoire, Gabon, Guinea, Luxembourg, Mali, Monaco, Niger, Senegal, Togo, Québec, and parts of Switzerland.

let's make...
ONION SOUP

This is very much an everyday soup. Most people grow a few onions in their yard, and every family has leftover bread that might be going stale. What better way to use it up?

WHAT YOU NEED:

SERVES 6 PEOPLE:

2 large onions
French country bread,
   a day or two old and
   perhaps a bit stale
4 ounces Cantal cheese,
   or Monterey Jack cheese
4 ounces Swiss Gruyère
   cheese
2 tablespoons duck
   or goose fat
salt, pepper

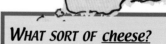

◁ This soup is very filling. Papa says people used to eat filling entrées and then only a morsel of meat. That's because meat was much more expensive.

WHAT SORT OF cheese?

This soup is traditionally made with two cheeses: Cantal from the Auvergne region in eastern France and Swiss Gruyère. Cantal has a strong, earthy flavor, a bit like Cheddar. You can use Cheddar or Monterey Jack instead. Gruyère is a great melting cheese. The stores may just call it "Swiss cheese."

1 Peel and finely chop the onions *(see page 5)*. Put the fat into a large saucepan and heat it over medium heat. Add the onions. Fry and stir them over gentle heat until they are a golden color.

!

2 Pour about 2–2½ quarts water into the saucepan. Season the soup generously with salt and pepper. Cover with a lid and cook the soup over gentle heat for about 25 minutes.

!

3 Roughly grate both cheeses. Cut the bread into thin slices. Heat the oven grill.

4 Place alternate layers of bread and cheese into a deep ovenproof soup bowl. Pour the soup into the bowl, over the bread and cheese layers.

5 Place the soup bowl under the grill and grill for about 5 minutes until the cheese melts. Stir the soup with a big spoon and serve at the table.

let's make...
40-CLOVE CHICKEN

That's clove as in "garlic clove!" We cook this dish quite often—and compete with the neighbors to see who will use the most garlic. Strangely, you can't smell it from miles away!

WHAT YOU NEED:

SERVES 4 PERSONS:

1 large chicken
   (about 3½ lbs)
salt, black pepper
½ bunch parsley
½ bunch thyme
40 garlic cloves (or roughly
   3–4 whole heads of garlic)
2 bay leaves
½ untreated organic lemon
4 tablespoons olive oil
1–2 cups chicken broth

◁ Once the garlic is cooked you can easily pop it out of its skin. My Gran serves this dish with toasted bread, and everyone "butters" their toast with the garlic pulp. Delicious!

HOW MUCH garlic?

The original French recipe speaks of *quarante gousses d'ail*, which means "40 garlic cloves." But there are other version with only 30 cloves, and also one with two whole strings of garlic heads! The exact number doesn't really matter. Cooking makes the garlic soft and mild in flavor. Just make sure there is plenty of it!

1 Wash the chicken and pat it dry with paper towels. Rub it inside and out with salt and pepper. Wash the herbs and shake them dry. Peel and roughly chop four of the garlic cloves *(see page 5)*.

!

2 Push the chopped garlic, bay leaves, parsley, half the thyme, and the half lemon into the chicken. Heat the oven to 450°F.

3 Pour the oil into a large Dutch oven. Place the chicken into the dish and turn it in the oil to coat it all over. Place the chicken breast side down.

4 Wash the remaining garlic heads with their skin on. Then cut each head in half (or separate out the cloves) and place them next to the chicken. Roast chicken and garlic for 30 minutes.

5 Turn the chicken over and pour the broth into the dish. Roast for another 30–40 minutes, or until the chicken is cooked.

6 Test if the chicken is done: prick the fattest part of a leg with a skewer and pull it out again. If the juices that flow out are pink, the chicken needs to roast longer. If they are clear, it is done. Serve with the roasted garlic.

!

let's make...
TARTE TATIN

This upside-down apple tart is totally delicious! It is served hot, straight from the oven, but it also tastes good cold. The tart can be made with other fruits, too.

WHAT YOU NEED:

MAKES 1 TARTE:

⅔ cup chilled butter
1⅛ cup plain flour (plus some more for the work surface)
1 pinch baking powder
2 tablespoons sugar
1 pinch salt
1 egg yolk
2¼ lb Golden Delicious apples
1⅛ cup confectioners' sugar

PLUS:
ovenproof pie dish (about 11 inches diameter)

◁ I love this tart piping hot with lots of vanilla ice cream. The contrast is delicious.

WHY IS IT CALLED: Tatin?

This tarte was invented by mistake: the Tatin sisters worked in a hotel in France. They were very busy, so they forgot to put the dough into the dish first when they were making an apple tart. But they had a great idea: they put the dough on top, cooked the tart like that, and then turned it all over. The guests loved it!

1 Cut ¼ cup butter into cubes. Knead the butter, flour, baking powder, sugar, salt, and egg yolk to a smooth dough. Shape this into a ball, wrap it in plastic wrap, and chill for 1 hour in the fridge.

2 Heat the oven to 450°F. Peel the apples and cut them into fourths. Cut out the cores. Sprinkle the base of the pie dish with the confectioners' sugar. Cook in the center of the oven for about 10 minutes, until the sugar is a golden caramel. Add the rest of the butter to the dish and let it melt. **!**

4 Meanwhile roll out the dough on a lightly floured surface, to make a circle a little larger than the pie dish. Take the dish out of the oven and turn the heat down to 400°F. **!**

3 Arrange the apple pieces with the rounded side down on top of the caramel. Bake for about 5 minutes in the center of the oven.

6 Take the tarte out of the oven. Get your assistant to help you with this: Place a large round platter on top and quickly turn both dish and platter over, holding them firmly together. Take off the pie dish and serve. **!**

5 Lift the dough onto the apples with the help of a rolling pin. Press down lightly around the edge. Prick the top several times with a fork. Bake the tarte for about 30 minutes.

Look it up
FRANCE

Armistice the end of a war; Armistice Day celebrates the end of World War I (1914–18) between the Allies and Germany on November 11

Bastille Day the French national festival on July 14; it celebrates the storming of the Bastille prison in Paris in 1789 and the beginning of the French Revolution

Caravane the convoy cars that advertise products ahead of the Tour de France cyclists

crêpe Suzette a sweet northern French pancake

croquembouche a French wedding cake; it is a tall pyramid of cream buns

French Revolution lasted from 1789 to 1799 and brought about major changes in French society; people rebelled because they wanted to rid themselves of a corrupt king and queen; this period ended when Napoleon came to power

gratin a dish cooked with cheese or cream that is cooked in the oven; it melts and has a crust; it often includes potatoes

méchoui a North African dish of (whole) marinated and barbecued lamb

pétanque a popular French game played with metal balls on a hard surface; the balls are thrown to be as close as possible to a smaller wooden ball, the jack

tarte tatin an upside-down cake with caramelized apples from central France; it is named after the sisters who invented it

Tour de France a French cycle race that lasts for three weeks and tours the entire country

Toussaint November 1, or All Saints' Day; it is celebrated by visiting the graves of the family dead

Victory Day May 8; on this day, French people celebrate freedom from German rule at the end of World War II (1939–45)

Find out more
FRANCE

Books to read

Fontes, Justine and Ron.
A to Z France (A to Z).
Children's Press, CT: 2004.

Landay, Elaine.
France (True Books).
Children's Press, CT: 2000.

Parks, Peggy J.
**A Taste of Culture – Foods of France
(A Taste of Culture).**
KidHaven Press: 2005.

McKay, Susan.
France (Festivals of the World).
Gareth Stevens Publishing: 1998.

Web sites to check out

**www.cia.gov/library/publications/
the-world-factbook/geos/fr.html**
The CIA's country listing on France, with
lots of facts and figures

www.www.francemag.co.uk
A site for all those who love France, with
food, drink, fashion, sports, history, art,
gardens, places to see, people gossip

**www3.nationalgeographic.com/places/
countries/country_france.html**
The National Geographic's site about
France, with information about history,
travel, flags, photographs

www.ambafrance-us.org/kids
The kids' pages of the Web site run by the
French Embassy in the United States

**www.oxfam.org.uk/coolplanet/ontheline/
explore/journey/france/frindex.htm**Infor
The Oxfam site, with lots of facts on
French culture, cooking, and scenery

Index
FRANCE